Season of renewal

a Lent course

by

Alison Morgan and Bill Goodman

Member's Coursebook

A ReSource publication

Renewal for mission in the power of the Holy Spirit

ReSource is a ministry with an Anglican distinctive, seeking to serve the church across denominations and traditions through teaching, training, and encouraging people to renew their lives and their church through the power of the Holy Spirit, so that God's message of life-changing love reaches out to others.

Published by:
ReSource
13 Sadler Street, Wells, Somerset BA5 2RR
office@resource-arm.net
www.resource-arm.net
Charity no. 327035

ISBN 978-1-906363-14-7

Acknowledgements

Unless otherwise stated, all Bible translations are taken from the New Revised Standard Version of the Bible, Anglicized edition, copyright © 1989, 1995 by the Division of Christian Education of the National Council of the Churches of Christ in the United States of America, and are used by permission. All rights reserved.

Photos on pp 13, 14, 23 © Alison Morgan. Photo on p 11 © Martin Cavender. Cover photograph © Alison Morgan.
Other images © iStockphoto.com (cover, pp 5, 12, 17), Fotolia (p 24).

Poem by RS Thomas © Kunjana Thomas 2001, from *Later Poems*, MacMillan1983
Poem by Susan Fisher reproduced from John Moses, *The Desert - an anthology for Lent*, Canterbury Press 1997
Poem by e.e.Cummings reproduced from *Selected Poems 1923-58*, Faber 1969.

Contents

How to use this coursebook

Season of Renewal is divided into six sessions - five for the five weeks between Ash Wednesday and Maundy Thursday, and one final session for the week after Easter, structured round a shared meal. Each session includes creative and practical elements as well as a focus on scripture and some times of prayer. We hope that participation in the course will bring about significant spiritual growth both for course members and in the life of the church of which they form part, and various suggestions are offered for how to maintain the impetus which has been created.

The course material is contained in a Leader's Manual. This member's Coursebook contains brief notes for each session and a pattern of spiritual exercises for you to follow during the week between meetings.

Season of Renewal : Introduction

Two thousand years ago, Jesus promised that through him we would find not just life, but abundant life. We live in a world which claims to offer us fulness of life, through material wealth and a culture of opportunity - but which often leaves us feeling dissatisfied, aware that there must be more to it than that.

Lent is a time in which traditionally we turn aside from the pursuit of material things, from the comfort of our modern lives, and seek to feed our souls with nourishment that is available to us only in Christ. It's a time which is often trivialised, reduced to the hopefully token giving up of this or that. And yet it's an opportunity to change gear for a while, to travel in company with one another on a different road - a less comfortable but ultimately more fulfilling road. It is our hope that this Lent course will enable you to do that, and to serve in some sense as a map for the journey.

What is Lent?

- Lent is a particular season

The early Christians fasted for one or two days just before Easter. This developed into a regular season of preparation for Easter, which became known in English as Lent (from the old English word for 'spring').

Many people today sense a real need to slow down, to rethink their commitments and priorities, to make time for reflection and prayer – but somehow they never get round to it. Lent offers an opportunity to do just that. It's in the calendar; the dates are already set, this course is being provided. Let's say to ourselves: 'Come to the spiritual feast – all is now ready!'

- Lent is a limited period

The traditional aim of Lent is to help believers rehearse the life of Jesus through their own prayers and actions, as a seasonal spiritual exercise which will draw us closer to God. It runs from Ash Wednesday, when we offer prayers of penitence and faith, to Easter Sunday, when we celebrate the new life which is ours through the death and resurrection of Jesus.

However, the fact that Lent is a limited period is also challenging. This group will not simply offer a warm, fuzzy experience; nor will it just drift aimlessly along. The aim is to allow God to change us for the better – both as individuals and together as a group or church. We seek a practical outcome by the end of this period. We look to God with eager expectation, at the same time as we look forward to the life-changing events of Easter.

* Lent is for all

From earliest times, Lent has been linked with baptism. New believers were instructed and prepared during Lent for their baptism at Easter. Lent also became a season for established believers to put on the armour of God and renew their spiritual life in disciplined prayer and repentance, leading to restoration of those who had fallen into sin and to a deeper level of fellowship and spiritual growth.

* Lent is a gift

Some people may remember the idea of 'giving up something for Lent' – a faint and rather feeble echo of the tradition of penitence. We may prefer the challenge to 'take up something for Lent', and particularly to take up this Lent course. Here is a gift which we can take hold of. But doing so may, of course, involve putting down something else – perhaps fasting from a favourite 'soap' or the Champions League on that particular night of the week!

What is the aim of this course?

The season of Lent runs for 40 days, modelled on the 40 days spent by Jesus in prayer and fasting following his baptism in the Holy Spirit. For Jesus, this period of prayer and fasting was a time of preparation for the three years of ministry which began immediately afterwards. So it is important for us to understand that taking Lent seriously may bring lasting personal change – Easter may be the end of a story, but it's also the start of a new and much bigger one. There's a lot more to Lent than giving up chocolate!

This booklet contains both a reminder of the material covered in the group session, and some suggestions for ways you can extend the session into your week. It is not a 'compulsory' part of the course to do these spiritual exercises, but we hope you will feel that you want to do them. You may wish to do them all, or you may prefer to choose one or two exercises each week and concentrate on those.

Whoever believes in me, as the Scripture has said, streams of living water will flow from within him.   John 7.38

Week 1 : Seasons of change

Exercise 1

One of the passages of scripture we looked at was **Psalm 104**. Read it again, slowly and reflectively. Take some time today to go for a walk in a park or through the countryside – or even round your own garden. Don't try to pray; just notice the details of the world God has made. Look for the first shoots of spring, or pause to take in a flower or berry. Look at the intricacy with which it has been made. Think about its place in what we rather boringly call the ecosystem, but which in the Middle Ages they used to call the 'Great Chain of Being'. How does God provide for this insect or flower?

Now think of yourself, and the world in which you live. How does God provide for you?

Thank him for his provision for you.

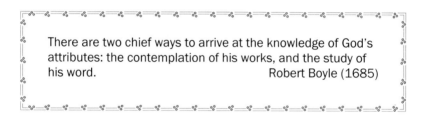

> There are two chief ways to arrive at the knowledge of God's attributes: the contemplation of his works, and the study of his word.
> Robert Boyle (1685)

Exercise 2

We also looked at **Ecclesiastes 3.1-15**. Read it again, slowly and reflectively.

We live in a world which is dominated by time. Some of us measure its progress on our wrists, run to keep up with it, despair at the speed of its passing. Others of us watch it stretch endlessly into a future which offers little to look forward to. Some of us try and cram as much as we can into it; others of us waste it or resent it.

What is your relationship with time? Think of your time as an offering to God. Remember that a minute lasts the same length of time however you spend it. Do you know that you can stop time? Try putting little intervals of quiet into your day – a few minutes here or there, when you say 'no' to the demands around you and focus on God. Don't feel you need to pray – just think about God, and how big he is, and how he has placed eternity inside you..

Perhaps you have not too much but too little to do. God is waiting for you. Read the poem again and ask, what is this time in your life for?

He has set eternity in the hearts of men.   Ecclesiastes 3.11 NIV

Exercise 3

Read **Jeremiah 17.7-8**:

> Blessed is the man who trusts in the Lord,
> whose trust is the Lord.
> He is like a tree planted by water,
> that sends out its roots by the stream,
> and does not fear when heat comes,
> for its leaves remain green,
> and is not anxious in the year of drought,
> for it does not cease to bear fruit.

Think back to the seasons exercise in the group meeting, and use this passage to think about your relationship with God. How deep are your roots? Are your leaves green? Does your spiritual life bear fruit in the lives of others?

Now read **Psalm 1**. This Psalm uses the same image of a tree, but makes a more specific link between spiritual vitality and the way in which we choose to live. Are there any things in your life which are preventing you from accessing the life-giving water which God has made available to you? In the Bible, water is often used as an image of the Holy Spirit. Do you feel that the Holy Spirit is with you, bringing new life to you as you depend on him?

Exercise 4

Lent is traditionally a time when we mark the seriousness of our intention to focus more on God by giving something up. It works as a kind of daily reminder. As you wait for the next group meeting, begin to think about whether there is anything practical you would like to do on a daily basis in order to remind yourself that you are asking for God's blessing on your life, and that you are ready to open yourself up to him and to the other members of the group to make this possible. Perhaps you could give up a particular television programme and use the time to do these exercises? Or you might get some ideas for something which has more of an outward focus by reading **Micah 6.8**, where the prophet declares that the best offerings are not material things but behavioural ones – ways of remembering God's care and compassion for us, and passing it on to others.

What does the Lord require of you but to do justice, and to love kindness, and to walk humbly with your God?   Micah 6.8

Exercise 5

One of the recommended lectionary readings for the second Sunday of Lent is **Psalm 27.** David was obviously finding life very difficult, and this psalm reads as a determined attempt to remind himself that he has genuinely and deliberately placed his trust God, and that this is what matters.

Read the psalm, and think about your own life. Ask yourself, are you able to pray this psalm with David, and to state that whatever may go wrong for you, you will remind yourself above all things that God is with you, and that you will experience his goodness?

Imagine yourself in God's shelter, or creeping into his tent, or standing high on a rock. Ask him to make you aware of his presence with you.

He will hide me in his shelter in the day of trouble; he will conceal me under the cover of his tent; he will set me high on a rock.   Psalm 27.5

Exercise 6

Think back over the week. What has changed for you in the course of the week? Are your hopes for the next few weeks still the same as they were in the first group meeting? Is there anything you would like to share with the other group members when you meet again?

Spend some time praying for the other members of the group, and especially for those who shared their pictures or poems with you. Ask the Lord to bless them and to draw close to them.

Pray too for the person leading the group, that he or she would know the peace of God as they prepare.

And pray for the next group meeting, that everyone would feel comfortable together, and that people would have the courage to be open with one another.

When it was evening.. Jesus came and stood among them, and said 'Peace be with you'.   John 20.21

Week 2 : Praying with Jesus

Exercise 1

Baptism is a sign of God's grace (God's generous love) to us, and our response to that grace.

Have you been baptised? If not, why not think about it and talk to one of the leaders in your church. If you were baptised as an infant, is now the time to be confirmed?

Look at these words, which come from the baptism service in Common Worship. Use them in your prayers this week, to recommit your life to Christ. Can you pray all these prayers without hesitation? If any of them seem particularly difficult to you, talk about it with a Christian friend.

In baptism, God calls us out of darkness into his marvellous light. To follow Christ means dying to sin and rising to new life with him. Therefore I ask

Do you reject the devil and all rebellion against God?   *I reject them*

Do you renounce the deceit and corruption of evil?   *I renounce them*

Do you repent of the sins that separate us from God and neighbour?
I repent of them

Do you turn to Christ as Saviour?   *I turn to Christ*

Do you submit to Christ as Lord?   *I submit to Christ*

Do you come to Christ, the way, the truth and the life?   *I come to Christ*

Exercise 2

Read **Mark 1.10** and **Mark 15.38**. These verses come at the beginning and end of Jesus' ministry on earth. In both cases the Holy Spirit comes. In both cases Mark talks about the heavens being torn. In Greek the verb is 'schizo', from which we get our words 'schizophrenic' and 'schism'. It's a violent, sudden verb - as if Mark is saying that there is now a hole torn in heaven, a hole which enables us to see through into a spiritual realm previously hidden to us. What does this mean for you? Do you have experience of this hole? You may like to pray that as you seek the presence of the Holy Spirit in your life you will become increasingly as much aware of spiritual reality as you are of the physical reality of the world around you. You may like to  write a poem or draw a picture of the tearing of the heavens; or to go for a walk and look for a break in the clouds and use it as a stimulus to your prayers.

It doesn't mean that Jesus saw a little door ajar miles up in the sky. It's more as though an invisible curtain, right in front of us, was suddenly pulled back, so that instead of the trees and flowers and buildings, or in Jesus' case the river, the sandy desert and the crowds, we are standing in the presence of a different reality altogether.   Tom Wright

Exercise 3

Read **Luke 4.1-2.**
Think about your experience of temptation. Most of us struggle with temptation in a particular area of life; for some it is money, for others anger, for others sex, or ambition, or pride... Do you know in which area the struggle is especially strong for you? Pray about that. Do you need to take some action to avoid particular temptations in that area? Do you need to talk about this with someone else?

Exercise 4

Read **Luke 4.3-14.** One of the ways in which Jesus resisted temptation was by knowing and using scripture (in this case, the book of Deuteron-omy). Do you read the Bible regularly? If not, why not start now! Read a few verses each day, and ask God to help you understand them and apply them to your life. You could start with one of the gospels. If you know a good Christian bookshop, visit it and ask about some of the

Bible reading aids which are available. Maybe a Christian friend can help and advise you as well.

Have you found any particular Bible verses helpful in dealing with temptation? If so, try learning a few by heart, one each week during Lent.

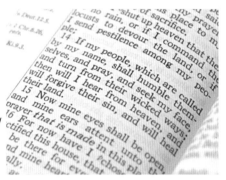

Exercise 5

Read **John 20.19-23**.
Spend some time sitting quietly in a chair. Rest your hands in a comfortable position on your lap, with palms facing down. Close your eyes. Breathe slowly and deeply. As you breathe out, think of the things you wish to give to God – burdens you need to shed, anxieties which worry you, failures in your life this week. Do this until you have handed these things to him.

Now concentrate on the breathing in. Keep the same slow rhythm. But this time, breathe in God's forgiveness and love. Breathe in God's peace, which Jesus promised to his frightened and confused disciples. Remember what this Bible word means:

- peace, harmony, tranquillity
- safety, welfare, health
- prosperity, well-being
- reconciliation
- wholeness
- flourishing
- salvation

Take these truths in, as you breathe in slowly and deeply. Turn your hands over so that the palms are facing upwards. Receive the Holy Spirit, who brings God's friendship and peace into your life.

Think of anyone you know who needs God's friendship and peace at the moment. Pray for them. Ask God to show you some way you might help them this week.

Psalm 51 - for meditation

Have mercy on me, O God, according to your steadfast love;
according to your abundant mercy blot out my transgressions.

Wash me thoroughly from my iniquity,
and cleanse me from my sin.

For I know my transgressions,
and my sin is ever before me.

Against you, you alone, have I sinned,
and done what is evil in your sight,

so that you are justified in your sentence
and blameless when you pass judgment.

Indeed, I was born guilty,
a sinner when my mother conceived me.

You desire truth in the inward being;
therefore teach me wisdom in my secret heart.

Purge me with hyssop, and I shall be clean;
wash me, and I shall be whiter than snow.

Let me hear joy and gladness;
let the bones that you have crushed rejoice.

Hide your face from my sins,
and blot out all my iniquities.

Create in me a clean heart, O God,
and put a new and right spirit within me.

Do not cast me away from your presence,
and do not take your holy spirit from me.

Restore to me the joy of your salvation,
and sustain in me a willing spirit.

Then I will teach transgressors your ways,
and sinners will return to you.

Deliver me from bloodshed, O God, O God of my salvation,
and my tongue will sing aloud of your deliverance.

O Lord, open my lips,
and my mouth will declare your praise.

For you have no delight in sacrifice;
if I were to give a burnt offering, you would not be pleased.

The sacrifice acceptable to God is a broken spirit;
a broken and contrite heart, O God, you will not despise.

Week 3 : All Things New

Exercise 1

Reflect on the following scriptures:

1 Peter 1.3 : Blessed be the God and Father of our Lord Jesus Christ! By his great mercy he has given us a new birth into a living hope through the resurrection of Jesus Christ from the dead.

2 Corinthians 5.17: So if anyone is in Christ, there is a new creation: everything old has passed away; see, everything has become new!

John 3.3 : Jesus answered him, "Very truly, I tell you, no one can see the kingdom of God without being born from above."

Psalm 104.30 : When you send forth your spirit, they are created; and you renew the face of the ground

Psalm 51.10 : Create in me a clean heart, O God, and put a new and right spirit within me.

Romans 12.1-2 : I appeal to you therefore, brothers and sisters, by the mercies of God, to present your bodies as a living sacrifice, holy and acceptable to God, which is your spiritual worship. Do not be con-formed to this world, but be transformed by the renewing of your minds, so that you may discern what is the will of God--what is good and acceptable and perfect.

2 Corinthians 4.16 : Even though our outer nature is wasting away, our inner nature is being renewed day by day.

Revelation 21.1-5 : Then I saw a new heaven and a new earth; for the first heaven and the first earth had passed away, and the sea was no more. And I saw the holy city, the new Jerusalem, coming down out of heaven from God, prepared as a bride adorned for her husband. And I heard a loud voice from the throne saying, "See, the home of God is among mortals. He will dwell with them as their God; they will be his peoples, and God himself will be with them; he will wipe every tear from their eyes. Death will be no more; mourning and crying and pain will be no more, for the first things have passed away." And the one who was seated on the throne said, "See, I am making all things new."

Lamentations 3.22-24 : The steadfast love of the LORD never ceases, his mercies never come to an end; they are new every morning; great is your faithfulness.

Exercise 2

One of the exercises in week 1 asked you to go for a walk in a park or countryside. Repeat that walk this week. This time, look out for signs of renewal – buds appearing on the trees; crocuses (perhaps even daffodils) pushing upwards. Here are new leaves and flowers, which have never seen the light of day before; yet they are not totally new – they come out of the old, the trees and bulbs which were already there.
Some bushes may have grown weaker, even died; some bulbs may have multiplied, bringing more blooms than last year.

Pray as you walk, offering yourself to God afresh - your unique personality with all its gifts, its strengths and weaknesses and potential. Ask God to bring new growth, fresh life and beauty out of you, in order to enrich the world around you. Be open to where this may lead you; perhaps letting go of some things in order for God to develop new life in other areas.

Exercise 3

Repeat what you did in the prayer time at the last session, when you reflected on Jesus' words 'Receive the Holy Spirit' and Paul's words 'be filled with the Spirit.' Pray for a fresh filling today for yourself, and for the others in the group.

Exercise 4

Have another look at the drawing of your spiritual journey which you began at the last group meeting. As you look back over your life so far, invite God the Holy Spirit to retrace the journey with you. This may bring to mind other details (people, events, experiences) which you want to add to the drawing.

Give thanks to God for all that you find in your drawing.

Exercise 5

Read **Galatians 5.22-25.**

During the last group meeting, we prayed for the presence and power of the Holy Spirit to come to us as a group and individually. In his letter to the Galatians, Paul describes some of the 'fruit' of the Holy Spirit. These are the beautiful and nourishing characteristics which God wants to grow in our lives as we open up to him.

Think back to the time when you first came to know Christ, or first took your spiritual life seriously. Has the fruit of the Spirit grown in you since that time? Thank him for helping you to become more like him.

Pray that the Lord would continue his work in you. Pray for any fruit which you would particularly like to see come to maturity, or which you find particularly hard to grow. You may find it helpful to think how this fruit was manifested in the life of Jesus himself, and meditate on that.

The fruit of the Spirit is love, joy, peace, patience, kindness, generosity, faithfulness, gentleness, and self-control.

Galatians 5.22-23

Week 4 : Depending on the Holy Spirit

Exercise 1

A church is a gathering of people 'called out' of the world to form a new community based on a shared relationship with Jesus Christ. It is not a building, or a certain way of doing things, or a set of values; the New Testament understands a church as an organic unity of individuals come together in a new way. Jesus invites us to consider ourselves as branches of a vine; Paul as parts of a human body.

Think back to the exercise where you identified which part of the body you would most like to use in the service of others in the church. Perhaps it was

- tongue for teaching or encouraging
- hands for healing, or practical tasks
- feet for walking alongside
- heart for caring
- arms for serving
- ears for listening

Pray that God would guide you as you look for an opportunity each day this week to do this. Ask him to send his Holy Spirit to bring life to and through what you offer to others in this way. Make time to think back over the day each evening, thanking him for what you have seen him do.

For we are what he has made us, created in Christ Jesus for good works, which God prepared beforehand to be our way of life.
Ephesians 2.10

Exercise 2

The New Testament talks about the gifts of the Holy Spirit – gifts that we give, gifts that we receive, even gifts that we ourselves become. All these gifts are given to bring life to our spirits so that we may build one another up.

Gifts that we give. These are described in **Romans 12**, and are often described as 'motivational' gifts because they motivate us to different forms of ministry; they are contributions which the Holy Spirit enables us to make to the church. The ministries Paul has in mind are preaching prophetically, serving others in practical ways, teaching and explaining things, encouraging others in their faith, giving financially, providing leadership, and offering compassion.

Gifts that we receive. Paul gives examples in **1 Corinthians 12**, and (as he did to the Romans) calls them 'charismata', things given by grace. These are mostly to do with specific kinds of help that we receive from the Holy Spirit as we pray, and they are exercised primarily for the benefit of others. Paul gives as examples wisdom, receiving words of knowledge, prophecy, faith, healing, miracles, the ability to discern spirits, to pray in tongues and to interpret tongues.

Gifts that we become. These are outlined in **Ephesians 4**, and they are to do with our roles. The word 'gift' in the Greek is different here from in the other lists – it's related to the word for 'dowry'. We ourselves are given in ministry to others. The main gifts Christ gives to his church are apostles, prophets, teachers, pastors, and evangelists.

Think about the church to which you belong. What kind of gift would you like to give, receive or become in your church? Think of yourself as a present, offering what you have received to others. What's inside? It may be something very grand or it may be something very practical – remember that practical presents are often the best ones! Be ready to share your thoughts in the group next week.

Exercise 3

Read **John 15.1-11**, where Jesus compares our relationship with one another and with him to the relationship the branches of a vine have with the vine itself (you may like to look also at Psalm 80, where the psalmist likens the people of God to a vine).

Think of the coming Spring. If you are able to, you may like to paint or draw a vine or other growing plant. You may prefer to take some photographs, or to go to a garden centre and buy a young plant or some seeds you can sow. But take the time to allow the creativity of God to be mirrored in you, and to pray that he would fill you with the life-giving sap which rises from the roots of the vine, so that you too may produce fresh leaves and fruits.

Exercise 4

One of the passages which may be read on Sunday during this week is **John 12.1-8**, which tells how Mary poured a whole jar of expensive ointment over Jesus' feet and then, not having a towel, wiped the excess off with her hair. John remembers that the whole room was filled with the scent.

As you continue to look for opportunities to minister to others this week, remember what Mary did that day. She had reason to be grateful to Jesus – she had seen him bring her dead brother Lazarus back to life. Remind yourself what it is that you are grateful to Jesus for. He is not physically present now, so you cannot show him your gratitude as Mary did - but he did say on another occasion that what we do for others, we do for him. Think of one thing you can do today for someone else to express your gratitude to Jesus.

> *I'm telling the solemn truth: Whenever you did one of these things to someone overlooked or ignored, that was me – you did it to me.*
> Matthew 25.40, The Message

Exercise 5

Read **John 20.19-23**. Pray as you prayed in exercise 5 of Week 2, sitting quietly and breathing slowly, using your hands to help you.

As you breathe out, think of the things you wish to give to God – burdens you need to shed, anxieties which worry you, failures in your life this week. Do this until you have handed these things to him.

Now concentrate on the breathing in. But this time, breathe in the peace of the Holy Spirit, the peace Jesus promised to his frightened and confused disciples. They were about to go and change the world. So are you, in your own way; for you too are part of God's plans. Breathe in slowly and deeply. Receive the Holy Spirit.

Now reflect. You have tried some new things this week. Which of them do you wish to make a permanent part of your life? Ask for his blessing and his guidance as you commit yourself to following his will.

You might like to pray this prayer written by Charles de Foucauld:

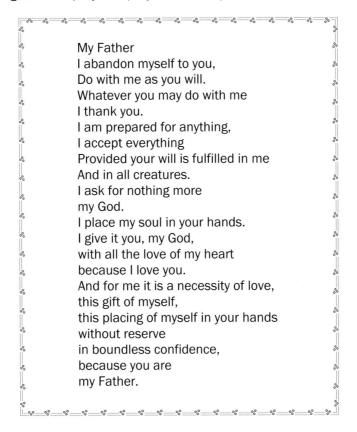

My Father
I abandon myself to you,
Do with me as you will.
Whatever you may do with me
I thank you.
I am prepared for anything,
I accept everything
Provided your will is fulfilled in me
And in all creatures.
I ask for nothing more
my God.
I place my soul in your hands.
I give it you, my God,
with all the love of my heart
because I love you.
And for me it is a necessity of love,
this gift of myself,
this placing of myself in your hands
without reserve
in boundless confidence,
because you are
my Father.

Week 5 : Made new for mission

Exercise 1

Read **1 Peter 2.4-10**. Think back over the last few weeks. What difference has the course made to your thinking and praying? How have things changed for you? Were there any key moments, either in the group meetings themselves or as you have worked through the weekly exercises at home? Do you feel that you are truly a living stone? Make a note here of the three things you most wish to carry forward with you:

1.

2.

3.

Exercise 2

Look at **Psalm 118**, which contains the verses Peter was referring to and which is set as a reading for the coming Palm Sunday. Thank God for sending Jesus and for making him the key stone in a new spiritual structure.

Now think again of **1 Peter 2**. What is your vision for the church as a spiritual house? Spend some time praying, and asking God to show you his hopes for your church. Make a note below of anything which comes to mind.

Exercise 3

Read **Luke 19.28-40**, which tells the story of Jesus' entry into Jerusalem. Jesus was riding into a city which he knew would welcome him only superficially. He knew that it was a place where God would not be recognised or honoured, and yet he was prepared to go there.

Now read **John 20.21**: 'As the Father has sent me, I am sending you'. Think of the community in which you live. Are you prepared to be sent like Jesus, to ride out like him from your safe places and take risks in order to make God known in your community? How can you and the church to which you belong minister as a holy priesthood to this community?

Try and think of one practical thing you can do this week to minister in some way to someone who does not know God. One thing, perhaps, that you could imagine Jesus doing.

The Church exists by mission, just as fire exists by burning.
Emile Brunner

Exercise 4

(This exercise is best done on Maundy Thursday).

Read **John 13.1-17**, which is the passage set for today. Washing someone's feet after a day's walking was the most practical thing you could do for them to demonstrate respect and concern. Sometimes we do it today as a spiritual exercise, but it can feel rather odd to remove the comfortable shoes and socks which keep our feet clean in order to do something we don't normally do for one another.

Can you think of a more effective way to wash someone's feet for them today, a way of doing something practical to make their journey through life a little easier?

Exercise 5

Read **Matthew 13.1-23**, which tells the story of the farmer sowing his seed.

Often we find that as we share our experience of what it means to be made new and to grow in Christ, people will rebuff us. Some, however, will not. Are you willing, like the farmer, to sow your seeds anyway?

Exercise 6

Using the clay which was given to you at the last meeting, make a model to represent anything which has inspired you as you have worked through the course. It could be something based on one of the illustrations, like the vine; something based on one of the exercises you have done together; something representing your vision of the future; something relating to your own prayer times as you have worked through the weekly exercises. Take your model to the shared meal so that you may all encourage one another.

The Holy Spirit did not come for our entertainment or excitement...
He filled the church so that the church might fill the world.
                                                      Simon Ponsonby

Seasons of renewal

Sometimes the landscape of my soul
seems like this burnt hillside,
the wind rattling orange leaves on black twigs,
the soil full of ash between the stones.
Sometimes the landscape of my soul
seems like this terrible waste of dead trees.

Walking this afternoon among the charred remains
I found a black stump sprouting leaves
and new grass thinly veiling
a delicate oak sapling
in this, the ravaged landscape of my soul.

Susan Fisher

And God held in his hand
A small globe. Look, he said.
The son looked. Far off,
As through water, he saw
A scorched land of fierce
Colour. The light burned
There; crusted buildings
Cast their shadows: a bright
Serpent, a river
Uncoiled itself, radiant
With slime.

On a bare
Hill a bare tree saddened
The Sky. Many people
Held out their thin arms
To it, as though waiting
For a vanished April
To return to its crossed
Boughs. The son watched
Them. Let me go there, he said.

R.S. Thomas

i thank You God for most this amazing
day:for the leaping greenly spirits of trees
and a blue true dream of sky;and for everything
which is natural which is infinite which is yes

(i who have died am alive again today,
and this is the sun's birthday;this is the birth
day of life and of love and wings:and of the gay
great happening illimitably earth)

how should tasting touching hearing seeing
breathing any - lifted from the no
of all nothing - human merely being
doubt unimaginable You?

(now the ears of my ears awake and
now the eyes of my eyes are opened)

e.e.cummings

About Alison Morgan

Revd Dr Alison Morgan is the author of *The Wild Gospel*, co-author (with John Woolmer) of the ReSource healing course *In His Name*, and the editor of the *Rooted in Jesus* discipleship course now in wide use in Africa. After 10 years on the staff of Holy Trinity, Leicester, she now works for ReSource as a thinker and writer.

About Bill Goodman

Ordained in 1989, Revd Bill Goodman worked in Anglican parishes in Burton-upon-Trent and Halifax for nine years. This was followed by six years in Ethiopia teaching at theological colleges in Addis Ababa and four years as Associate Minister of Holy Trinity, Leicester. Now studying for a PhD, he is also a member of the ministry team at St Wilfred's, Kibworth.